Grow Towards the Sun

Jing Wu

a DSTL arts publication

Grow Towards the Sun

a DSTL Arts publication

The work in this book was written by Jing (Heidi) Wu, a participant in DSTL Arts's Poet/Artist Development Program, and first printed in March, 2024 by DSTL Arts publishing in Los Angeles, CA, U.S.A.

Cover Design: Luis Antonio Pichardo

Book Design: Luis Antonio Pichardo

ISBN: 978-1-946081-71-1

10 9 8 7 6 5 4 3 2 1

www.DSTLArts.org

DSTL
arts

Los Angeles, CA

Dear Reader

I wrote these poems for you. When I started writing, I didn't realize that my English was growing and improving. After more than two years of writing in English, I have found that my poetry is still blossoming and it is the result of more than 20 years of learning English.

As a little girl, born and raised in China, I faced numerous challenges in learning English. However, I refused to let these difficulties deter me from my dream of writing. Through my perseverance and dedication, I was able to find my voice as a poet.

You may not fully comprehend the challenges I have faced as a non-native English speaker. Nonetheless, I implore you to cherish this book and savor each poem quietly. While my English may not be perfect, my emotions and intentions are genuine. I believe you will find nourishment in these poems and they will help to enrich your life.

Thank you for taking the time to read my work.

Sincerely,

Jing (Heidi) Wu
Your soulful author

Day and Night
—To my teacher, Mrs. Rivers

In the morning,
the sun shines through a small crack in the window.
I know
I should get up.
I hear Mrs. River's voice,
"Heidi, get up
and go to school.
I'll wait for you in the classroom."
At night,
the sun sets in the valley,
and I need to go home to sleep,
like the sun!

Contents

Grow Towards the Sun

I Am From a Small Town

I.

I am from a small town;
I am a small-town girl;
even if you use the largest map of China,
you are also hard to find;
in ancient legends,
there was a small cave where rice flowed out every day;
but greedy people were digging holes every day;
then one day, the small cave became a big cave;
people found the rice no longer flowed,
only a quiet stream flowed from the cave.

I am from a small town;
I am a small-town girl;
the town has no trains, no cars, no subways,
only the ferry for residents to travel on the water;
even if the town does not have modern facilities,
people who love beauty use plants to decorate their lives
until one day, the town becomes a beautiful sea of flowers;
people find that life no longer needs material abundance;
all it takes is the abundance of the spiritual world.

I am from a small town;
I am a small-town girl;
the town is a Utopia,

with no complicated interpersonal relationships;
only unity and friendship;
I am from a small town;
I am a small-town girl;
I have never been ashamed of my birth;
I appreciate this vast world from the perspective of a small-town girl.

II.

I am from a small town;
I am a small-town girl;
first arrived in the city,
I am lost at an intersection with traffic lights,
red light, green light, yellow light,
should I go left or right?
fear and shyness haunt me;
should I be brave or cowardly?
girls call me "Country Girl";
I wonder;
city girl, country girl?
Is there a difference?
I have too many questions;
the question mark is like a hat,
wear it on my head anytime, anywhere;
like a troubled teenager,
I fear I'll end up on the street;
I lose myself,
I struggle,
I fight;
I don't want to be swallowed by the city;

I don't want to drown in tall buildings;
I make myself an invisible woman
to disappear into the crowd.

III.

I am from a small town
where everyone knows my name,
where fields stretch on for miles
and life is a simple game.

I am a small-town girl,
with dreams as big as the sky;
I want to spread my wings
and learn to soar up high.

But now I am in the city
and everything's so new;
I am lost in the hustle-bustle
of this world that's not so true.

The traffic lights confuse me;
red, green, and yellow too;
I am not sure where to go
or what I am supposed to do;
the city girls are different,
their clothes, their hair, their ways;
they don't understand my country roots
and how I've spent my days.

I won't let that stop me;

I'll learn to find my place
and though I miss my small town,
I won't forget my roots, my grace.

For though I may be lost,
and the city may seem big,
I'll keep my small-town heart
and spread my wings to live.

IV.

I am from a small town,
where life moves at a gentle pace,
where neighbors lend a hand
and smiles light up each face.
I am a small-town girl,
with dreams that reach the sky;
I want to see the world
and watch the stars up high.

But now I am in the city
and it's a different scene;
the lights are bright and flashing
and people move like machines.
I miss the sound of crickets
and the smell of fresh-cut hay,
but I'll embrace this new adventure
and see where it leads today.

I'll learn to navigate the streets
and make friends along the way;

I'll keep my small-town values
and let them guide me each day.

For though the city may be big
and life may move so fast,
I am a small-town girl at heart
and that's the strength that lasts.

So I'll keep my head up high
and chase my dreams with all my might;
I am from a small town,
the world within my sight.

V.

I am a small-town girl;
where the air is fresh and clean,
where the pace is slow and steady
and the streets are rarely seen.

I am a small-town girl,
with a heart full of hope and joy;
I want to see the world
and find my place to deploy.

But now I am in the city
and it's a different kind of place;
the sounds and smells are foreign
and the people have a different face.

I miss the simple pleasures,

like stargazing at night
or walking through the fields
and watching birds take flight.

I'll embrace this new adventure
and see where it may lead;
I'll learn to navigate the city
and find the things I need.

I am a small-town girl,
with a heart that's pure and kind;
I'll take on the challenges
and leave the past behind.

I'll make new friends and memories,
find my place in the city;
I am from a small town,
but my spirit is free and gritty.

VI.

I am from a small town,
but now I am in the city;
this fast-paced lifestyle
is taking hold of me completely.

My hometown is a blur
as the city has taken root;
the hustle-bustle of it all
has become my new pursuit.

I run to keep up
with the pace of this new life,
but I worry about growing up
and losing sight of what's right.

The label "country girl"
feels like a distant past;
as I try to keep up
with this city's frantic blast.

I don't have time to think
or to feel sad or glad
as everything is moving
fast, fast, fast.

But in the midst of all this rush,
I've lost my sense of self;
I can't even find my way,
or know where to turn for help.

The small-town girl in me
feels like a thing of the past,
but maybe it's time to slow down
and let those memories last.

For though this city may be grand
and everything moves so fast,
I'll always be from a small town,
a part of me that will last.

Lotus Pond Moonlight

On a summer night so bright,
I stroll by my alma mater's lotus pond in delight;
in the moon's ambiguous light,
the lotus pond gleams, a wondrous sight.

During the day, I study with all my might,
no time to admire the lotus in the sunlight;
I rush past the pond on my way
to the dining hall, classroom, or library to stay.

A nerdy existence some may say,
reading and studying day after day,
but in the stillness of the night,
my heart awakens to a new delight.

I close my eyes and breathe in deep
the air so fresh, my soul takes a leap;
and when I open them again,
the lotus pond shines with a new sheen.

Emerald leaves and pink petals so fine,
a fairy-like temperament, so divine;
under the cover of night
the lotus pond takes on a magical light.

Intoxicated by its refined grace,
I linger by the pond, that serene space;

the lotus pond, a hidden treasure,
a true delight beyond all measure.

I Am a Lucky Girl

I am a lucky girl,
endowed with tenacious vitality;
I survived childhood hunger,
adolescent school violence
and the challenges of youth wandering;
I refused to be swallowed
by the mortal dust of this world
or lost in the brutality of humanity;
I chose to embrace innocence, kindness, toughness,
the pillars of my existence in this world.

I am a fortunate girl,
a zealous learner, hungry for knowledge;
I study hard every day, every moment,
even when it means drinking water instead of eating;
I became a sponge, crazed in the ocean of knowledge,
absorbing nutrients to erase poverty, backwardness, and ignorance;
learning is the only weapon
that sets me apart from others.

I am a lucky girl
blessed with the courage to be kind;
leaving home at a young age exposed me to bullies,
but I refuse to believe that all humans are bad.
weakness is insurmountable in some,
but my heart will go on, even in the toughest of times;

I still believe
I am a lucky girl;
this belief has sustained me so far
and I invite you to glimpse into my heart
to hear the voice that drives me.

What Is a Beautiful Day?

Birds singing in the morning light,
I take a walk by the lake;
nature surrounds me with delight.

The birds' sweet melodies fill the air
as I greet them on my way;
"Good morning, Heidi, how do you fare?"
the birds seem to ask and say.

"My day is beautiful, thank you," I reply.
"Your singing makes it even better."
The birds soar and fly,
a sight that leaves me in wonder.

Their song echoes in the sky
as they're asking me once more,
"What is your beautiful day?" they imply,
and I answer, "Birds singing and more."

Both Sides of the Creek

Flowers on the far side of the creek,
their colors so vibrant and sleek;
I run to see, but as I peek
they fade away, elusive and meek.

Mountains on the other creekside;
a gust of wind brings a tale to confide
of times and moments that abide
in memories that we hold inside.

Birds on the far side of the creek
up early every day to speak
with melodies that are unique,
a joyous chorus, ever antique.

Gorgeous clouds on the other creekside
look back as if they want to hide
and miss everything in the world besides
their beauty, elusive and dignified.

Sunshine on the other creekside
from the mountaintop to the valley wide
falls like a waterfall in a playful stride
on the grass, sparkling and glorified.

Lotus Flower in a Lotus Pond

Lotus, green stems
on the green torus
supporting white and pink flowers.

Lotus, white petals, with a bit of pink
looks like a girl in first love,
in sweet shyness
revealing the taste of happiness.

Lotus, like summer,
blooming on hot summer days;
green rhizomes,
turning into a white lotus root.

Lotus, likes to be lined with big, velvety leaves,
the leaf likes rolling dewdrops,
drop by drop,
crystal clear water droplets
flowing on the green lotus leaves
like summer flowing in my heart.

In the Fields

I ran in the fields;
the fragrance of the earth was refreshing;
I ran in the fields;
the yellow wildflowers swayed and smiled at me;
I ran in the fields;
the unfolding voice relaxed me;
I ran in the fields;
the heavy rice in autumn bent over like a smile.

I ran in the fields;
going back to the joyous, happy days of childhood,
I ran in the fields;
the earth hugged me like a mother listening
to my childlike crying;
I ran in the fields;
the setting sun and the hills on the horizon
merged into one.

I ran in the fields;
the green broad-bean leaves opened like a
mouth and laughed at me;
I ran in the fields;
the chubby baby opened his mouth and smiled at me;
I ran in the fields;
two birds flew side by side with beautiful feathers,
a loving couple;

I ran in the fields;
the setting sun guided me home.

Riverside

I grew up by the riverside,
where the water meanders far and wide,
a tranquil and silent place to be,
where ships and stories pass by me.

I sit upon the pier with ease,
watching ships sail with the breeze,
I ponder on the passengers' tales,
wondering what their story entails.

I want to hear their stories told,
emotions and feelings so bold;
each person a protagonist in my mind,
their tales so vivid and intertwined.

Some say I have a writing gift,
but it's this river that gives me a lift,
a flowing stream that inspires me each day,
a muse that won't let my ideas stray.

As long as I'm by the river's flow,
my writing will never slow;
it will continue to be endless and true,
thanks to this river and its calming hue.

Autumn Wind

I stroll through autumn's golden days
as leaves rustle in the autumn wind's soft ways;
it whispers in my ear, so near,
"Heidi, write me a poem, my dear."

"Why should I?" I ask with a grin;
the wind replies, "Or winter will begin,"
but I am no longer young and spry;
just a little haste makes me sigh.

"I cannot write the poem you seek,
so go away and let me be," I speak;
the wind sighs and moves away,
leaving me to ponder and sway.

I miss the half-green, half-yellow leaves
and the golden rice waving in the breeze;
I miss the sweet persimmons and pumpkins, too
and all the wonders autumn can imbue.

The autumn wind whispers again,
"Don't be afraid, my dear friend.
I will come again next year;
be here and wait without fear."

Self Struggle

When the wrinkles in my heart
surpass those on my face,
I know I'm tired,
exhausted and drained of grace.

I can't complain about fate's injustice
or life's many hardships,
but I long for rest and respite,
even as I keep fighting.

My birth was just a starting point,
lower than most, but still a chance;
I chose to begin at the bottom
among society's cruel and ugly stance.

I am like a fish in muddy waters,
adapted to survive and thrive
as long as I have food and air,
I'll push through and stay alive.

I don't know how the struggle will end
or what it may ultimately mean,
but as long as I have breath to live,
I'll keep striving to be my best, unseen.

Lost Dreams

My dreams, a piece of paper in my backpack;
holding my memories, I took them to a new land,
but the wind, a gentle gust, took them away,
along with my laughter, lost in the sand.

The light in my eyes, the memories dear;
an eternity it seems, but now out of sight;
the paper, an address, my parents' home so near;
blown away, like a kite without a string to take flight.

My heart feels empty, a part of it gone;
the dreams I had, faded paper to me;

floating away, I watch them as they move on,
lost in the wind, no longer mine to see.

Female Warrior

From childhood to adulthood,
I've lived as a female warrior;
every day fighting like a man,
running around to make a living,
facing the hardships of life,
making my voice louder
and my appetite grew stronger.

Sometimes, I wonder,
am I truly a woman or a man?
Only in the dead of night
do I allow myself to cry,
teeth clenched,
quilt pressed against my face
trying to stifle the sound,
wondering why fate has been so unfair,
forcing me to live like a man.

But I cannot afford to dwell on this,
for tomorrow morning brings a new battle
and I must rise like a female warrior once more;
put on my armor, and charge forth,
with courage and determination
to conquer the challenges that lie ahead.

I Am a Little Blade of Grass

I am a blade of grass, small and green,
born in the high mountains, rarely seen;
I lack the height of the mighty trees
and the fragrance of flowers on the breeze.

I am never lonely or in despair;
my grassy friends are everywhere;
the spring breeze makes me dance and sway;
the sun's warmth helps me grow each day.

The rivers flow and paint me green;
the mountains rise and make me keen
to absorb the nutrients from the earth
and grow stronger with every birth.

Now, the earth and sky embrace me tight;
I am no longer a blade in the night;
I have become a well-known grass,
with a mind as strong as my body mass.

Though I was once unknown and small,
now a famous blade standing tall,
grateful for Mother Earth's tender care,
I'll be a seed, her love to share.

A World of Birds and Flowers

I adore the butterflies dancing in spring;
I cherish the cicadas singing in summer's swing;
I relish the harvest of fruits and melons in fall
and the quietness of winter's snow enthralls.

As a child, I savored nature's bountiful pleasure,
but as I grew, I saw a world that changed with measure;
we humans treat nature with rough hands,
fishing, hunting, and polluting our lands.

The fish that swim and spawn in rivers, lakes, and seas
are mercilessly hunted, with no thought to species;
we dump garbage in the oceans, polluting marine life,
killing sea turtles, who consume plastic in strife.

Nature is sad and angry, with humans' endless demands;
its anger turns to storms, ravaging the land;
the storms are its tears, extreme weather their wrath;
humans remain blind and deaf, walking a different path.

Nature hopes to see humans' fear of death,
the damage caused to our planet's breath;
reflect on our mistakes and stop blaming each other
and cherish the world, our home, like a lover.

Nature is calling, with its birds and flowers
reminding us to cherish its gifts and powers;
the warm sunshine, fresh air, and clean water,
let us return to nature, be one with its charter.

I Am a Quiet Woman

I am a woman from the ancient East;
outwardly calm, but wild within;
I crossed the ocean to chase my dreams,
but Oriental culture dampened my hopes.

The oppression of women stifled me;
I couldn't breathe, suffocated by tradition;
I longed for the fresh air of freedom,
for a life unrestrained, unburdened.

The road ahead is tough, but I cannot turn back;
looking back on my life, I know one thing for sure;
I am a quiet woman, keeping my words close,
choosing my own path and living recklessly.

Like a kite soaring freely in the sky,
I revel in the exhilaration of living
as a quiet woman unbound by fear or doubt.

Wildflower

I am a wildflower that grows in the mountains,
standing tall on a cliff, blooming with pride;
I breathe in the fresh air of the mountains,
drawn to the aura that surrounds me outside.

My leaves, a vibrant emerald green,
my flowers, pure white, with golden stamens seen;
nature gives me good nutrients to thrive,
so I blossom where I am, grateful to be alive.

Never do I think to leave my rocky base,
for this is where my roots are strong and secure;
transplant me to a pot and I wither without a trace
or pluck me from my home, and my beauty is no more.

I don't seek to be picked or placed in a vase;
my place is in the wild, where I am free,
where the soil is rich and the water is pure,
where I belong, just a wildflower being me.

Standing On a Mountain

I ascend to the mountain's peak
sensing everything beneath my feet;
clouds drift like cotton on the slope;
the sun is so close, I can almost cope;
all becomes surreal, magical, and grand,
as if strength is infused through my hand.

Though I have not changed anything,
I never underestimate the mountain's power;
its presence humbles and makes me feel alive;
awe-inspired, I cherish this moment, this hour.

Standing on the top, I feel empowered,
like I'm at the summit of my life;
gazing at the horizon, feeling showered
by nature's wonders, free of strife.

Four Seasons Movement

I wander through the vibrant spring;
the aroma of blossoms fills my soul;
butterflies dance around me, taking a swing,
higher and higher, till everything's a blur;
whispers of the wind
searching for lost kites;
one lost kite
stuck in a tree, couldn't resist.

I stroll through the scorching summer.
heat pressing down on me,
I dive into the water;
emerging, still steaming,
I gaze up;
the sun blazing overhead
sizzling me with its hot glare;
popsicle in my hand
melting from the summer's stare.

I stride through the colorful autumn;
persimmons orange-red and falling,
wheat stalks golden bowing,
maple leaves red;
earth is decorated with grace,
green leaves clinging, unwilling to shed,
half yellow, half green, a beautiful face;

I lose myself in
charming autumn's embrace.

I meander through the splendid winter;
white snow everywhere and bare trees,
but in my eyes, a lonely, beautiful plum blossom,
tenacious and brave, blooming with ease,
I don't want to hibernate in winter's bosom,
so I light a heart lamp to gaze at the four seasons' motion.

Castle in the Sky

The sky, a canvas of soft blue
reflects the mountain's verdant hue,
but high-rise buildings stand in lieu
of empty lands where nature grew.

Who spilled the painter's palette here?
The world is now so bright and clear,
red flowers, green trees, pink and peer
purple butterflies, free to veer.

Yet, something's off, the sky's not soft;
the green is not the green aloft;
no fish swim in the clear, once oft,
now just lazy people, sweet and soft.

Ascetic

I am an ascetic from the East,
my path is one of piety and peace,
with a sign on my chest to remind me,
pedestrians, who pass me by,
that I seek truth and scriptures divine.

No water, no food, it doesn't matter,
for I am determined to reach the altar;
I wear a tattered cassock and broken shoes;
under the scorching sun, I walk with purpose and muse.

No one cares about my journey or strife,
but I single-mindedly seek a higher life;
I embrace the hardships and the pain,
for only through suffering can true wisdom be gained.

I am not here to escape reality,
but to seek truth and live a life of clarity;
I do not want to lose myself in pleasures or gain;
I seek the essence of East and West
to save the ignorant of the world from pain.

I am an ascetic who sails on wind and waves;
no water, no food, only scriptures to save;
my journey is one of self-discovery and light,
for I am determined to reach enlightenment's height.

The City

The city looms like a colossal ghost,
tall buildings of concrete and steel;
a beast that devours human souls,
absorbing their vitality, making them kneel.

Those who come to the city to survive
are like grains thrown into a cement mixer
crushed into bits, no matter how hard they strive,
their native land is a dream, the city a fixer.

The city offers no sympathy, no respite;
throwing everyone under the weight of life;
in cramped apartments, the people unite,
packed like sardines, no escape from strife.

Endless work, overtime, and strife
in exchange for a living space the size of a matchbox,
one careless move can shatter your city dream,
but there's nowhere to run, no key to the lock.

The hometown dream cannot be revived;
the city is a deep abyss, a never-ending grind,
a sacrifice made for the next generation to survive,
even in death, the dream remains unlined.

The cemeteries cost more than rent;
the city's thirst for blood knows no relent.

Chinese White Porcelain Bowl

That white porcelain bowl
is like my love;
It joins me every day
holding my food,
even listening to me talk.

I brought It from the East,
to this new coast,
although our lives have changed,
It remains steadfast and constant.

It once held rice, dumplings, and noodles,
but now It holds pasta,
hamburgers, pizza, and fries;
It reminds me to be mindful of my stomach,
warning me about the dangers of soda.

During Chinese New Year,
It prompts me to make dumplings,
reminding me of my identity and past,
of childhood memories and loved ones,
filling my eyes with tears.

It doesn't share my grief,
but It is like me,

a symbol of hope in a bowl,
a familiar memory.

I thought to replace It with plates,
knives, and forks,
but It reminded me we are part of a dynasty,
a period of history that cannot be rewritten.

So, I keep It with me
forever in my life,
because It is an antique,
a vessel of my memories.

The Miracle of Friends

Everyone needs a friend,
for we fear being alone;
a friendless existence
is like a lonely soul
dancing the tango in an empty sky.

A life without friends
is like a man shipwrecked on an island,
lonely, helpless, in despair;
no one enjoys this feeling.

A friend is like a lifeline
held by a drowning man,
a connection not to be easily let go.

Friends are like mountain streams
offering warmth and care
easily flowing into people's hearts.

The process of finding a friend
is like a treasure hunt;
you never know who
will become your best friend.

Sometimes, a friend without blood ties
can be closer than a relative;
this feeling is mysterious

and who can fully understand
the miracle of friendship?

Love and Marriage

Falling in love may be easy,
but staying married is tough;
this truth is known to all,
yet, it can't stop us humans
from pursuing love and its call.

Even if marriage is the end of love,
people are drawn like moths to a flame;
marriage can feel like a siege;
some hope to break free from their chains,
while others strive to enter its realm
to conquer it like a warrior in a game.

Choosing the right path isn't easy;
we must wait to see what happens;
accept it with open arms;
love and marriage are adventures in life,
meant for human reproduction or desire,
each person's answer varies. It's rife.

I Want to Compare You to Spring

I want to compare you to Spring;
like a willow tree by the lake,
you sway gracefully,
bringing joy to those around you.

I want to compare you to Spring;
I see you blooming;
I don't see you falling;
you are always alive,
with fresh green climbing your branches.

I want to compare you to Spring;
wherever you go, you fascinate me;
blossoming everywhere,
Spring is pink and willow green.

I want to compare you to Spring;
the moonlight is bright and gentle;
you are my response,
always there to bring light to my life.

Be Yourself

I often stand in front
of the mirror and ask
myself three
philosophical questions,

"Who are you?"

"Where are you from?"

"Where are you going?"

I dare not stare at
myself in the mirror;
I'm afraid

of wrinkles rising from
the corners of my eyes;
I'm afraid

of the growing lines and
folds around my mouth;
I'm afraid

the uneven teeth are
getting thinner;
every day, I am afraid

of the shifting hairline, daily

hair loss;
I am afraid

aging will take over my body;
I fear the power of fear
overcoming my strength.

Be yourself; how easy
is it for someone born
in an authoritarian state?

Everyone must live
a lie, can't tell the truth;
you must live with a mask,

a fake smirk speaking
false words in exchange
for the right to live;

be yourself
is the biggest lie.

Are you talking about feminism?
It's not that
men don't want

to give it to you, because
men have no human rights
too.

Me Too

The world was born unfair.
As women, we are told
we are nothing but a man's rib,
taught to depend on men to survive;
our destiny is to return to the family,
be a good wife and mother;
our educational goal is to find the right match,
not to increase knowledge or gain a career;
our degrees on display next to family albums;
we return home to become free babysitters
for a warm family harbor,
but our hands on keyboards turn into toilet tools,
our introverted sense of loss flows like a toilet's running water,
no one cares, no one respects;
for the long-term, unpaid domestic labor
we are family volunteers
giving without expecting anything in return
until the marriage falls on the verge of breaking;
no one seeks justice and no union can recover
the unpaid labor after labor;
we question in the dead of night;
looking in the mirror, asking ourselves,
"If there is an afterlife,
 do we want to be a woman again?"
 but the mirror silently responds
 with an empty wall, no answer is given.

Roots

Humans, like plants,
need roots to grow and thrive,
but the life of immigrants
is like a rootless plant.

We grew up in our homeland
surrounded by familiar sights and sounds,
the care of our parents and the love of our kin,
gave us the fertile soil we needed to flourish.

Leaving behind the familiar,
we are airdropped into an unfamiliar land
overwhelmed and apprehensive;
we fear the unknown future that lies ahead.

We mourn the loss of familiar faces and places,
the flavors of our childhood,
the warmth of our community.

Adapting new cultures and languages,
forging new friendships;
everything is new, unfamiliar.

The pain of loss and fear of the future
seep into our bones and our hearts,
a constant reminder of challenges we face.

We are like rootless duckweed

drifting aimlessly,
with no roots to lean on.

But we persevere, work hard
and slowly, we find a place to belong.

We may never forget the pain of uprooting,
the loss of familiar soil,
but we will find a way to grow new roots,
and thrive once more.

I Am a Creek

I am a creek born in the mountains high,
yearning for the vast and boundless sky;
no longer content to stay in the stream,
I dash ahead with all my strength and gleam.

Through moss-covered canyons and winding caves,
I travel great distances, rippling on pebbled waves;
people pass by my bridge and flowing water,
bid me farewell in every season, every quarter.

In spring, I sing the song of new beginnings;
green trees and red flowers bloom beside me, winning;
dancing gracefully on the hillside, I sway,
rejoicing in the warmth of the sun's rays.

In summer, I sing the melody of life,
mountain flowers on the shore, free from strife,
exuding a charming fragrance, I roll
in the beauty of nature, serene and bold.

In autumn, I sing the hymn of change,
red maple leaves, painting the world in range;
vibrant with the vitality of the season,
I embrace the beauty of life's every reason.

In winter, I sing of pure white,
a thousand miles of frozen delight;

white snowflakes flutter, creating
a world of poetry and awakening.

Year after year, day after day,
I journey on without delay
and when cicadas sing in summer's heat,
I finally merge with the ocean complete.

Now, I am the vast and boundless sea,
a new beginning, wild and free.

Go Home

Walking on a foreign road,
fragrant breeze in my nose,
sunshine caressing my face,
but my heart is always morose.

People say it's a good place;
life seems peaceful and serene,
but my mind keeps wandering back
to the place where I have been.

In the daytime, I remind myself,
this is my new home to stay,
but at night I can't resist
longing to be far away.

Oh, hometown, how I miss thee;
my heart aches with every beat;
you're etched deeply in my soul
and with you I want to meet.

Let's go home without delay;
don't wait for success or fame;
no longer afraid to return empty-handed
to our parents, we'll proudly proclaim.

We'll pack our bags and leave right now,
not letting our wandering steps stray;

our restless hearts will no longer roam,
to home, we'll find our way.

Go home;
don't stop for a moment;
pack your bags and go now;
just for the wandering footsteps not to lose their way
only the wandering heart will no longer wander;
Go home;
Don't stop for a moment;
Pack your bags and go now...

Life, Sand, Castle

I see my life as a sand castle
built on a beach of shifting sand;
each time I add a little more,
a wave comes and washes it away.

I build it up again and again,
only to see it crumble once more;
a never-ending cycle of hope and loss,
of sadness and grief that fills my mind.

But still, I rise again and again,
determined not to give up or give in,
to cross the ocean of fate and chance
and change the course of my life.

Someday, I'll add some rocks and stones,
and build my castle tall and strong,
a testament to perseverance and will
for the world to see and know I've lived.

Life may be like the sand on the shore,
ever-changing and hard to endure,
but I will keep building my castle
and show the world what I'm made of.

My Heart is Often a Gallery

My heart is often a gallery,
memories both bright and dull;
some bring smiles, some bring tears,
sometimes I don't know which is which.

There is laughter, there is pain;
joy and heartache coexist;
pictures on the wall
remind me where I stand.

But though my heart may be a place
for memories of the past,
I know I can do more
to create a brighter future.

For every painting that hangs there,
is a story untold;
I can add my own chapters;
let it be bold with love and joy.

So I'll embrace this gallery,
this home of memories;
try to make it brighter
with love and happiness, tapestry.

I Am a Little Dandelion

I am a little dandelion,
with a white and light body;
fly, fly, I dream of flying, fly, fly, fly,
ready to take off and fly;
I wait for the wind, my friend,
to carry me up high.

I have no wings, it's true;
the blue sky is my closest friend,
the earth my final resting place,
but the wind helps me soar
across fields and over hills
to places I've not seen before.

I spread my seeds on my journey,
planting hope with every flight
and when the wind dies down,
I rest on petals glowing bright;
stored energy
waiting for the next time I fly again,

I am a little dandelion
dreaming of the endless sky
where I dance with other seeds;
help me plant the seeds of new hope;
as we float and flutter by,
It carries me far away,

So let the wind come and take me
to new adventures yet to be;
It will be a sky full of dandelions flying,
I love starting the journey of my dreams;
I am a little dandelion...
with a spirit wild and free.

Sweet Night Dream

The night sky opens up before me,
a stillness that soothes the soul;
a sprinkle of starlight like fine silver
glimmering amidst the darkness whole.

A meteor flashes, adding life to the night
like spring sprouts and summer cicadas;
autumn fruit and winter plum blossom,
nature's symphony plays its melodious cadence.

In the deep of the night, the sky turns darker,
becomes a canvas of boulders, tranquil yet stark
as if a band is playing in the distance,
each note soars higher, soars far.

Together, with the starlight they create
a name for the night woven by their fate
and in the distance, a mountain's outline,
moonlight and a gentle wind, a sweet design.

They accompany me into my sweet dreams,
a peaceful slumber, so it seems,
a tranquil journey, a moment of delight
as I drift into the land of the night.

About the Author

I was born in the most remote town in Northwest China; its name is Donghe Town. When I was a child, my parents had to leave their hometown to work full-time. Without friends, I grew up alone. I learned to read and write. Writing is like the continuous circulation of blood in my body.

I had the opportunity to move to Beijing, the capital of China, to spend my teenage years growing up, and even in China, I was an immigrant. In 2018, I had the opportunity to come to the United States to start my new life, which inspired my dream of writing in English. I hope to keep writing and give back to everyone who helped me.

I'm working on my second book of poetry "Echoes of Home: Heidi's Poems", and working on a Chinese-English bilingual children's picture book titled "Jing and An". The book features Chinese twins who may look alike but have distinct personalities that celebrate diversity and show that differences are valuable.

DSTL
arts

This publication was produced by DSTL Arts.

DSTL Arts is a nonprofit arts mentorship organization that inspires, teaches, and hires emerging artists from underserved communities.

To learn more about DSTL Arts, visit online at:
DSTLArts.org
@DSTLArts

www.ingramcontent.com/pod-product-compliance
Lightning Source LLC
Chambersburg PA
CBHW060427090426
42734CB00011B/2483